MINIMALIST LIVING

Embracing Simplicity in a Complex World

SREEKUMAR V T

FOREWORD

In a world that often equates success with accumulation and complexity, the concept of minimalist living stands out as a refreshing and transformative alternative. "Minimalist Living: Embracing Simplicity in a Complex World" is a beacon of light in our modern age, offering a profound invitation to re-evaluate our priorities and embrace a life of greater meaning and fulfilment.

This book is not just about decluttering our physical spaces, although that is certainly a part of it. It is about decluttering our minds, our schedules, and our lives as a whole. It is about stripping away the unnecessary and focusing on what truly matters, so that we can live with greater intention and purpose.

Through practical advice, inspiring stories, and thoughtful reflections, "Minimalist Living" shows us how to simplify our lives in a way that is both meaningful and achievable. From re-evaluating our possessions to reimagining our goals, this book offers a roadmap to a more intentional and fulfilling life.

As you embark on this journey of minimalist living, I encourage you to approach it with an open mind and a willing heart. Embrace the simplicity and clarity that comes from living with less, and discover the joy and freedom that comes from focusing on what truly matters.

SREEKUMAR V T

COPYRIGHT WARNING

CONTENTS

1. THE ESSENCE OF MINIMALISM

Understanding the Philosophy

In a world filled with constant noise and distractions, the concept of minimalism emerges as a guiding principle for living a more intentional and meaningful life. At its core, minimalism is not just about decluttering our physical spaces; it is a philosophy that encourages us to simplify every aspect of our lives, from our possessions to our schedules to our mindset.

At the heart of minimalism lies the recognition that our culture often equates success with accumulation: more possessions, more responsibilities, more commitments. However, this relentless pursuit of more can leave us feeling overwhelmed, stressed, and disconnected from what truly matters.

Minimalism invites us to challenge this mindset and ask ourselves: What do we truly value? What brings us joy and fulfilment? By decluttering our lives and focusing on the essentials, we create space for the things that truly matter.

Minimalism is not about deprivation or austerity; it is about consciously choosing to live with less in order to create a life of greater meaning and purpose. It is about aligning our actions with our values and prioritizing the things that bring us true happiness.

In this book, we will explore the various facets of minimalist living, from decluttering our physical spaces to simplifying our schedules to cultivating a minimalist mindset. We will discover how minimalism can help us reduce stress, increase our productivity, and find greater contentment in our everyday lives.

As we embark on this journey toward minimalist living, let us embrace the philosophy of less is more and discover the profound joy that comes from embracing simplicity in a complex world.

2.THE BENEFITS OF MINIMALIST LIVING

Why Less is More

In a world that often celebrates excess and accumulation, the concept of minimalist living offers a refreshing alternative. Minimalism is not just about decluttering our physical spaces; it is a mindset that can transform every aspect of our lives. By embracing minimalism, we can experience a wide range of benefits that can improve our overall well-being and quality of life.

In this article, we will explore the numerous benefits of minimalist living, from reducing stress and anxiety to increasing our focus and productivity. We will also discuss how minimalism can help us cultivate a deeper sense of gratitude and contentment in our lives.

Reduced Stress and Anxiety

One of the most significant benefits of minimalist living is the reduction in stress and anxiety that it can bring.

Cluttered and chaotic environments can contribute to feelings of overwhelm and anxiety, while minimalist spaces promote calmness and clarity. By simplifying our surroundings, we can create a more peaceful and serene environment that can help us relax and unwind.

Improved Focus and Productivity

A cluttered environment can also impair our ability to focus and concentrate. Minimalist living encourages us to eliminate distractions and focus on the task at hand. This can lead to increased productivity and efficiency in our work and personal lives. When we are not surrounded by unnecessary distractions, we can devote more time and energy to the things that truly matter.

Financial Freedom

Minimalism can also lead to greater financial freedom. By embracing a minimalist lifestyle, we can reduce our expenses and live more frugally. This can free up resources that can be used to pursue our passions and goals. Additionally, minimalism can help us break free from the cycle of consumerism and the constant desire for more. Instead of accumulating possessions, we can focus on experiences and relationships that bring us true happiness.

Environmental Benefits

Minimalist living is also beneficial for the environment. By consuming less and reducing waste, we can minimize our impact on the planet. Minimalism encourages us to buy only what we need and to choose products that are durable and sustainable. This can help reduce our carbon footprint and contribute to a more sustainable future.

Cultivating Gratitude and Contentment

Minimalist living can also help us cultivate a deeper sense of gratitude and contentment. When we have fewer possessions, we learn to appreciate what we have more fully. We are less likely to take things for granted and more likely to savour the simple pleasures in life. This can lead to a greater sense of fulfilment and happiness in our lives.

In conclusion, minimalist living offers a wide range of benefits that can improve our overall quality of life. From reducing stress and anxiety to increasing our focus and productivity, minimalism can help us lead more intentional and fulfilling lives. By embracing the philosophy of less is more, we can create a life that is simpler, more meaningful, and more aligned with our values.

3.DECLUTTERING YOUR PHYSICAL SPACE

Simplify Your Environment

In today's fast-paced world, our lives are often cluttered with an excess of possessions. From clothes we never wear to gadgets we rarely use, our homes can easily become overwhelmed with stuff. This clutter not only takes up physical space but also mental and emotional energy. However, by embracing minimalist principles and decluttering our physical spaces, we can create a more peaceful and harmonious environment that fosters clarity, creativity, and contentment.

The Benefits of Decluttering

Decluttering your physical space offers a wide range of benefits that can positively impact your life in numerous ways:

1. **Reduced Stress**: A cluttered environment can lead to feelings of overwhelm and anxiety. By decluttering, you create a more serene space that promotes relaxation and reduces stress.

2. **Increased Productivity**: Clutter can be distracting, making it difficult to focus on tasks. A tidy space allows for greater concentration and efficiency.
3. **Improved Mood**: A clean and organized environment can have a positive effect on your mood, helping you feel more calm and content.
4. **Enhanced Creativity**: Clutter can stifle creativity by overwhelming the senses. A minimalist environment fosters clarity of thought and allows for more creative thinking.
5. **Better Health**: Clutter can contribute to allergies and other health issues. Removing clutter can improve air quality and create a healthier living environment.

Getting Started with Decluttering

Decluttering your physical space can seem like a daunting task, but it doesn't have to be overwhelming. Here are some tips to help you get started:

1. **Set Clear Goals**: Determine what you want to achieve through decluttering. Whether it's creating a more organized space or reducing the number of possessions you own, having a clear goal will help you stay motivated.
2. **Start Small**: Begin decluttering one area at a time, such as a closet or a single room. Breaking the process down into smaller tasks makes it more manageable.
3. **Declutter Ruthlessly**: Be honest with yourself about what you truly need and use. If an item no longer serves a purpose or brings you joy, it may be time to let it go.
4. **Organize as You Go**: As you declutter, take the time to organize the items you decide to keep. Invest in storage solutions that help you maintain a tidy space.
5. **Maintain Regularly**: Once you've decluttered and organized your space, make an effort to maintain it on a regular basis. Set

aside time each week to tidy up and prevent clutter from building up again.

Decluttering your physical space is a powerful way to simplify your life and create a more peaceful and harmonious environment. By letting go of excess possessions and organizing your space mindfully, you can enjoy the numerous benefits of minimalist living. Start small, set clear goals, and embrace the process as a journey toward a more simplified and fulfilling life.

4.MINIMALIST DESIGN

Creating a Calm and Functional Home

I n a world that often feels chaotic and overwhelming, our homes should serve as sanctuaries of peace and tranquility. Minimalist design offers a path to creating a space that is not only aesthetically pleasing but also promotes a sense of calm and functionality. By embracing minimalist principles in our home decor, we can cultivate a living environment that enhances our well-being and supports our lifestyle.

The Principles of Minimalist Design

Minimalist design is characterized by simplicity, functionality, and a focus on essential elements. It emphasizes the idea that less is more, encouraging us to pare down our belongings and create a space that is free from unnecessary clutter. Key principles of minimalist design include:

1. **Simplicity**: Minimalist design is all about simplicity. It involves stripping away excess decoration and focusing on clean lines and uncluttered spaces.
2. **Functionality**: A minimalist home is designed to be highly functional, with each piece of furniture and decor serving a specific purpose.
3. **Quality over Quantity**: Rather than filling your home with numerous items, minimalist design emphasizes the importance of choosing quality pieces that will stand the test of time.
4. **Clutter-Free Spaces**: Clutter is the enemy of minimalist design. A minimalist home is free from unnecessary objects, creating a sense of openness and tranquility.
5. **Neutral Color Palette**: Minimalist design often relies on a neutral color palette, such as whites, grays, and earth tones, to create a sense of serenity.

Benefits of Minimalist Design

Embracing minimalist design in your home can offer a wide range of benefits, including:

1. **Reduced Stress**: A clutter-free environment can help reduce feelings of stress and anxiety, promoting a sense of calm and relaxation.
2. **Increased Productivity**: A minimalist workspace can help you stay focused and productive by eliminating distractions.
3. **Improved Mood**: A clean and organized home can have a positive impact on your mood, helping you feel more content and at peace.
4. **Enhanced Creativity**: A minimalist environment can stimulate creativity by providing a clear and uncluttered space for ideas to flow.
5. **Better Quality of Life**: By simplifying your living space, you can create a more enjoyable and fulfilling home environment that supports your well-being.

Tips for Creating a Minimalist Home

Creating a minimalist home is a process that takes time and effort, but the results are well worth it. Here are some tips to help you get started:

1. **Declutter Regularly**: Begin by decluttering your home and getting rid of items you no longer need or use.
2. **Choose Quality Over Quantity**: Invest in high-quality furniture and decor that will last for years to come.
3. **Keep It Simple**: Stick to a neutral colour palette and avoid overly decorative elements.
4. **Embrace Negative Space**: Leave plenty of empty space in your home to create a sense of openness and calm.
5. **Organize Thoughtfully**: Use storage solutions to keep your home organized and free from clutter.

Minimalist design offers a powerful way to create a home that is both beautiful and functional. By embracing the principles of simplicity, functionality, and quality, you can create a space that enhances your well-being and supports your lifestyle. Whether you're looking to reduce stress, increase productivity, or simply create a more peaceful home environment, minimalist design can help you achieve your goals. Start small, declutter regularly, and embrace the beauty of minimalist living in your home.

5.DIGITAL MINIMALISM

Reducing Screen Time and Information Overload

In today's digital age, we are constantly bombarded with information and distractions from our electronic devices. While technology has brought many benefits to our lives, it has also created a sense of overwhelm and distraction that can detract from our well-being. Digital minimalism offers a way to reclaim control over our digital lives and reduce the negative effects of excessive screen time and information overload.

Understanding Digital Minimalism

Digital minimalism is a philosophy that advocates for a mindful approach to the use of technology. It is based on the idea that we should be intentional about how we use our devices, focusing on what adds value to our lives while minimizing distractions. Key principles of digital minimalism include:

1. **Mindful Consumption**: Digital minimalism encourages us to be mindful of the content we consume online, focusing on quality over quantity.
2. **Reduced Screen Time**: Digital minimalism emphasizes the importance of reducing screen time and setting boundaries around device use.
3. **Digital Decluttering**: Just as we declutter our physical spaces, digital minimalism encourages us to declutter our digital spaces by removing apps, emails, and files that no longer serve a purpose.
4. **Quality Connections**: Digital minimalism emphasizes the importance of cultivating meaningful connections online and offline, rather than seeking validation through social media.

Benefits of Digital Minimalism

Embracing digital minimalism can offer a wide range of benefits, including:

1. **Improved Focus**: By reducing distractions and limiting screen time, digital minimalism can help improve focus and concentration.
2. **Reduced Stress**: Excessive screen time and information overload can contribute to feelings of stress and overwhelm. Digital minimalism can help reduce these negative effects.
3. **Increased Productivity**: By focusing on what truly matters and eliminating distractions, digital minimalism can help increase productivity and efficiency.
4. **Better Mental Health**: Excessive screen time has been linked to poor mental health outcomes. Digital minimalism can help improve mental health by encouraging a more balanced approach to technology use.
5. **Enhanced Creativity**: Digital minimalism can stimulate creativity by providing space for reflection and contemplation, free from constant digital stimulation.

Practical Tips for Practicing Digital Minimalism

Practicing digital minimalism doesn't mean completely eliminating technology from your life. Instead, it's about finding a balance that works for you. Here are some practical tips for practicing digital minimalism:

1. **Set Boundaries**: Establish limits on your screen time and stick to them. Consider using apps or settings that track your usage and help you stay within your limits.
2. **Declutter Your Digital Space**: Regularly go through your apps, emails, and files and delete anything that no longer serves a purpose.
3. **Unplug Regularly**: Set aside time each day to unplug from your devices and engage in activities that don't involve screens.
4. **Curate Your Digital Life**: Be selective about the content you consume online and the people you interact with. Focus on quality over quantity.
5. **Practice Mindfulness**: Be mindful of your digital habits and how they impact your well-being. Pause before reaching for your phone and ask yourself if the activity is truly adding value to your life.

Digital minimalism offers a way to regain control over our digital lives and reduce the negative effects of excessive screen time and information overload. By practicing mindfulness and setting boundaries around our technology use, we can create a more balanced and fulfilling relationship with technology. Whether you're looking to improve focus, reduce stress, or enhance creativity, digital minimalism can help you achieve your goals and live a more intentional life in a complex digital world.

6.SIMPLIFYING YOUR WARDROBE

The Capsule Wardrobe Approach

In a world where fast fashion and trends change rapidly, maintaining a clutter-free and functional wardrobe can be a challenge. The capsule wardrobe approach offers a solution to this problem by advocating for a minimalist and intentional approach to clothing. By curating a collection of versatile and timeless pieces, you can simplify your wardrobe, reduce decision fatigue, and cultivate a more sustainable and mindful approach to fashion.

What is a Capsule Wardrobe?

A capsule wardrobe is a curated collection of essential clothing items that can be mixed and matched to create a variety of outfits. The concept was popularized by fashion designer Donna Karan in the 1980s and has since gained traction as a sustainable and minimalist approach to dressing. The key principles of a capsule wardrobe include:

1. **Quality Over Quantity**: A capsule wardrobe focuses on investing in high-quality, durable pieces that will last for years to come, rather than buying cheap, disposable clothing.
2. **Versatility**: The items in a capsule wardrobe are carefully selected to be versatile and interchangeable, allowing for a wide range of outfit combinations.
3. **Timelessness**: A capsule wardrobe consists of timeless, classic pieces that transcend trends and can be worn season after season.
4. **Minimalism**: The goal of a capsule wardrobe is to streamline your closet and eliminate excess, focusing on only the items that you truly love and wear regularly.

Benefits of a Capsule Wardrobe

Embracing the capsule wardrobe approach offers a wide range of benefits, including:

1. **Simplicity**: A capsule wardrobe simplifies your morning routine by reducing decision fatigue and making it easier to put together outfits.
2. **Clutter-Free Closet**: By curating a smaller, more intentional wardrobe, you can eliminate clutter and create a more organized and visually appealing closet.
3. **Cost-Effective**: While investing in high-quality pieces for a capsule wardrobe may initially seem expensive, in the long run, it can save you money by reducing the need for frequent shopping and impulse purchases.
4. **Sustainable Fashion**: By focusing on quality over quantity and wearing your clothes for longer, you can reduce your environmental impact and contribute to a more sustainable fashion industry.

5. **Personal Style**: A capsule wardrobe encourages you to define your personal style and curate a wardrobe that reflects your unique tastes and preferences.

How to Create a Capsule Wardrobe

Creating a capsule wardrobe is a process that involves careful planning and curation. Here are some steps to help you get started:

1. **Assess Your Current Wardrobe**: Start by taking stock of your current wardrobe and identifying pieces that you love and wear regularly, as well as those that no longer serve a purpose.
2. **Define Your Style**: Consider your lifestyle, personal style, and the occasions you dress for. Choose pieces that reflect your style and can be mixed and matched to create a variety of outfits.
3. **Choose Versatile Pieces**: Select pieces that can be worn in multiple ways and paired with different items in your wardrobe. Look for neutral colors and classic silhouettes that can be easily mixed and matched.
4. **Limit the Number of Items**: While there is no set number of items for a capsule wardrobe, aim to keep it relatively small and manageable. A typical capsule wardrobe may consist of 30-40 items, including tops, bottoms, dresses, and outerwear.
5. **Rotate Seasonally**: Update your capsule wardrobe seasonally to accommodate changing weather and trends. Store off-season items in a separate space to keep your closet clutter-free.

A capsule wardrobe offers a minimalist and sustainable approach to dressing that can simplify your life and elevate your style. By curating a collection of timeless and versatile pieces, you can create a wardrobe that reflects your personal style, reduces decision fatigue, and contributes to a more sustainable fashion industry. Whether you're looking to streamline your closet, save money, or reduce your environmental impact, the capsule wardrobe approach can help you achieve your goals and embrace a more mindful approach to fashion.

7.MINDFUL CONSUMPTION

Making Conscious Choices

In a world driven by consumerism and the relentless pursuit of more, mindful consumption offers a refreshing alternative. It is a practice that encourages us to be conscious and intentional about the things we buy and consume, with a focus on quality over quantity. By embracing mindful consumption, we can reduce waste, minimize our environmental impact, and cultivate a more meaningful and fulfilling life.

Understanding Mindful Consumption

At its core, mindful consumption is about being aware of the impact of our purchasing decisions on ourselves, others, and the planet. It involves considering the ethical, environmental, and social implications of what we buy and consume, and making choices that align with our values and priorities. Key principles of mindful consumption include:

1. **Conscious Awareness**: Mindful consumption begins with being mindful of our thoughts, emotions, and motivations when it comes to buying and consuming goods and services.

2. **Intentional Choices**: Mindful consumption involves making deliberate and thoughtful choices about what we buy, focusing on what we truly need and value.
3. **Quality Over Quantity**: Mindful consumption emphasizes the importance of choosing quality products that are built to last, rather than buying cheap, disposable items.
4. **Sustainability**: Mindful consumption considers the environmental impact of our purchasing decisions, and seeks to minimize waste and support sustainable practices.
5. **Gratitude**: Mindful consumption encourages us to cultivate a sense of gratitude for the things we have, rather than constantly seeking more.

Benefits of Mindful Consumption

Embracing mindful consumption offers a wide range of benefits, both for individuals and for society as a whole:

1. **Reduced Clutter**: By being mindful of what we buy and consume, we can reduce clutter in our homes and create a more organized and peaceful living environment.
2. **Environmental Impact**: Mindful consumption helps reduce waste and minimize our carbon footprint, contributing to a healthier planet.
3. **Financial Savings**: By focusing on quality over quantity and avoiding impulse purchases, mindful consumption can save us money in the long run.
4. **Improved Well-being**: Mindful consumption encourages us to prioritize experiences and relationships over material possessions, leading to greater overall satisfaction and well-being.
5. **Social Responsibility**: Mindful consumption supports ethical and sustainable practices, and can help create a more equitable and just society.

Practical Tips for Practicing Mindful Consumption

Practicing mindful consumption doesn't have to be complicated. Here are some simple tips to help you get started:

1. **Buy Only What You Need**: Before making a purchase, ask yourself if the item is something you truly need or if it's just a want.
2. **Quality Over Quantity**: Invest in high-quality items that are built to last, rather than buying cheap, disposable products.
3. **Research Before You Buy**: Take the time to research products and companies to ensure they align with your values and priorities.
4. **Avoid Impulse Purchases**: Before making a purchase, take a moment to pause and consider if it aligns with your values and if you really need it.
5. **Practice Gratitude**: Cultivate a sense of gratitude for the things you have, rather than constantly seeking more.

Mindful consumption is a powerful practice that can help us live more intentionally and sustainably. By being conscious of our purchasing decisions and making choices that align with our values, we can reduce waste, minimize our environmental impact, and cultivate a more meaningful and fulfilling life. Whether you're looking to declutter your home, save money, or make a positive impact on the planet, mindful consumption offers a path toward a more sustainable and mindful way of living.

8.MINIMALIST MEAL PLANNING

Simplifying Your Diet

I n our fast-paced world, meal planning can often feel like a daunting task. However, by embracing minimalist principles, we can simplify our approach to meal planning and create a more sustainable and enjoyable eating experience. Minimalist meal planning is about more than just simplifying your recipes; it's about making conscious choices that prioritize health, sustainability, and enjoyment. In this article, we will explore the benefits of minimalist meal planning and provide practical tips for simplifying your diet.

The Benefits of Minimalist Meal Planning

Minimalist meal planning offers a wide range of benefits that can positively impact your health, well-being, and lifestyle. Some of the key benefits include:

1. **Saves Time**: By planning your meals in advance, you can save time during the week and reduce the stress of last-minute meal

decisions.

2. **Reduces Food Waste**: By planning your meals based on what you already have and buying only what you need, you can reduce food waste and save money.
3. **Promotes Healthier Eating Habits**: By focusing on simple, whole foods, minimalist meal planning can help you make healthier food choices and improve your overall diet.
4. **Saves Money**: By planning your meals and shopping strategically, you can save money on groceries and reduce the temptation to eat out.
5. **Promotes Mindful Eating**: By taking the time to plan and prepare your meals, you can cultivate a greater appreciation for food and practice mindful eating.

Practical Tips for Minimalist Meal Planning

1. **Start with a Menu Template**: Create a simple menu template for the week, including breakfast, lunch, dinner, and snacks. This will help you stay organized and avoid last-minute decisions.
2. **Focus on Simple Recipes**: Choose recipes that require minimal ingredients and preparation time. Look for recipes that can be easily modified to suit your preferences and dietary needs.
3. **Use What You Have**: Take inventory of your pantry, fridge, and freezer before planning your meals. Try to use ingredients you already have on hand to reduce waste and save money.
4. **Plan for Leftovers**: Cook larger batches of meals and plan for leftovers. This will save you time and ensure you have healthy meals available throughout the week.
5. **Shop Wisely**: Make a list of the ingredients you need before going to the store and stick to it. Avoid impulse purchases and try to buy in bulk when possible to save money.
6. **Embrace Seasonal Eating**: Plan your meals around seasonal produce to save money and enjoy the freshest ingredients.
7. **Keep It Simple**: Don't overcomplicate your meals. Focus on simple, nutritious ingredients and let the flavours speak for themselves.

Minimalist meal planning is about more than just simplifying your diet; it's about making conscious choices that prioritize health, sustainability, and enjoyment. By embracing minimalist principles and simplifying your approach to meal planning, you can save time, reduce waste, and improve your overall health and well-being. Whether you're looking to save money, eat healthier, or reduce your environmental impact, minimalist meal planning can help you achieve your goals and embrace a simpler, more mindful approach to eating.

9.STREAMLINING YOUR FINANCES

Living Within Your Means

In a world where consumerism and materialism often drive our spending habits, it can be challenging to maintain a healthy financial outlook. However, by embracing minimalist principles and streamlining your finances, you can take control of your money and live a more fulfilling and stress-free life. This article will explore the concept of minimalist finance, offer practical tips for simplifying your financial life, and provide guidance on how to live within your means.

Understanding Minimalist Finance

Minimalist finance is about more than just budgeting and saving money; it's about aligning your financial goals with your values and priorities. It's about living intentionally and making conscious choices about how you earn, spend, and save your money. At its core, minimalist finance is about living within your means and finding contentment with what you have, rather than constantly striving for more.

The Benefits of Streamlining Your Finances

Streamlining your finances offers a wide range of benefits that can positively impact your life in numerous ways:

1. **Reduced Stress**: By simplifying your finances, you can reduce the stress and anxiety that often come with managing money.
2. **Financial Freedom**: Living within your means allows you to break free from the cycle of debt and financial insecurity, giving you greater freedom and control over your life.
3. **Increased Savings**: Streamlining your finances can help you save more money, allowing you to build a financial cushion for emergencies and future goals.
4. **Improved Relationships**: Money is a common source of tension in relationships. By streamlining your finances and aligning your goals, you can improve communication and harmony in your relationships.
5. **Environmental Impact**: Minimalist finance encourages conscious consumption, which can reduce your environmental impact and contribute to a more sustainable lifestyle.

Practical Tips for Streamlining Your Finances

1. **Create a Budget**: Start by creating a budget that outlines your income, expenses, and savings goals. This will help you understand where your money is going and identify areas where you can cut back.
2. **Simplify Your Accounts**: Consolidate your bank accounts and credit cards to make managing your finances easier. Consider automating your bills and savings to avoid late fees and ensure you're consistently saving money.

3. **Cut Back on Expenses**: Identify non-essential expenses that you can eliminate or reduce. This could include dining out less frequently, cancelling subscriptions you don't use, or finding cheaper alternatives for things like groceries and entertainment.
4. **Prioritize Your Spending**: Focus on spending money on things that bring you true value and happiness. Consider adopting a "one in, one out" rule for new purchases to avoid clutter and impulse buying.
5. **Build an Emergency Fund**: Aim to save at least three to six months' worth of living expenses in an emergency fund. This will provide you with a financial safety net in case of unexpected expenses or job loss.
6. **Invest Wisely**: Consider investing in assets that align with your long-term financial goals and risk tolerance. Diversifying your investments can help protect your wealth and ensure long-term growth.

Streamlining your finances is an essential step toward embracing a minimalist lifestyle and living within your means. By simplifying your financial life, you can reduce stress, improve your financial security, and align your spending with your values and priorities. Whether you're looking to save more money, reduce debt, or achieve financial freedom, embracing minimalist finance can help you achieve your goals and live a more intentional and fulfilling life.

10. MINIMALIST PARENTING

Raising Children with Less

P arenting in the modern world comes with its own set of challenges, not the least of which is the constant barrage of messages telling us that more is better. More toys, more activities, more stuff. But what if we flipped that script? What if, instead of trying to do and have it all, we embraced a more minimalist approach to parenting?

Minimalist parenting is about more than just decluttering your child's toys or simplifying their schedules (though those are certainly part of it). It's about intentionally choosing to focus on what truly matters, and letting go of the rest. It's about creating a calm, nurturing environment for your child to grow and thrive, free from the distractions of excess stuff and over-scheduled days.

The Principles of Minimalist Parenting

Minimalist parenting is guided by several key principles:

1. **Intentionality**: Minimalist parents are intentional about the choices they make for their children. They focus on what is truly important and let go of the rest.
2. **Quality Over Quantity**: Minimalist parents prioritize quality time and experiences over the accumulation of material possessions.
3. **Simplicity**: Minimalist parents strive to simplify their children's lives, reducing clutter and avoiding over-scheduling.
4. **Mindfulness**: Minimalist parents practice mindfulness in their parenting, paying attention to their child's needs and emotions.
5. **Presence**: Minimalist parents prioritize being present with their children, putting away distractions and giving their full attention.

Benefits of Minimalist Parenting

Minimalist parenting offers numerous benefits for both children and parents:

1. **Less Stress**: By simplifying their lives, minimalist parents can reduce stress and create a more peaceful home environment.
2. **Stronger Relationships**: Minimalist parenting encourages deeper connections between parents and children, fostering stronger relationships.
3. **Improved Focus**: Minimalist parenting helps children focus on what is truly important, leading to better concentration and academic performance.
4. **Financial Savings**: By avoiding the trap of consumerism, minimalist parents can save money and teach their children the value of money and possessions.
5. **Environmental Impact**: Minimalist parenting reduces waste and consumption, leading to a smaller environmental footprint.

Practical Tips for Minimalist Parenting

1. **Limit Toys**: Instead of overwhelming your child with toys, focus on a few high-quality, open-ended toys that encourage

imaginative play.
2. **Simplify Activities**: Avoid over-scheduling your child with extracurricular activities. Instead, focus on a few activities that they truly enjoy and benefit from.
3. **Create Routines**: Establishing simple routines can help children feel more secure and reduce meltdowns.
4. **Model Minimalism**: Children learn by example, so model minimalist behaviour by simplifying your own life and possessions.
5. **Focus on Experiences**: Instead of material possessions, prioritize experiences that create lasting memories for your child.

Minimalist parenting is about more than just decluttering your child's toys or simplifying their schedules. It's about embracing a mindset that values quality over quantity, mindfulness over busyness, and presence over distractions. By adopting a minimalist approach to parenting, you can create a more peaceful, intentional, and fulfilling family life for you and your children.

11.MINIMALISM IN RELATIONSHIPS

Cultivating Meaningful Connections

I n our fast-paced, consumer-driven society, it's easy to get caught up in the pursuit of more: more possessions, more experiences, more connections. However, the essence of minimalism teaches us that less can often be more, especially when it comes to our relationships. Minimalism in relationships is about focusing on quality over quantity, cultivating meaningful connections, and decluttering our social lives to make room for what truly matters. In this article, we'll explore the principles of minimalist relationships, the benefits they offer, and practical tips for cultivating more meaningful connections in your life.

Principles of Minimalist Relationships

Minimalist relationships are guided by several key principles:

1. **Quality Over Quantity**: Minimalist relationships prioritize quality connections over a large number of superficial relationships. It's about investing time and energy into relationships that are meaningful and fulfilling.
2. **Intentionality**: Minimalist relationships are intentional. They require us to be mindful of the relationships we cultivate and to actively choose to invest in those that bring value to our lives.
3. **Simplicity**: Minimalist relationships are simple. They are free from drama, competition, and unnecessary complexity. They focus on the core elements of connection: communication, understanding, and support.
4. **Authenticity**: Minimalist relationships are authentic. They are built on honesty, openness, and genuine care for one another. There is no pretense or facade, just a real and meaningful connection.
5. **Boundaries**: Minimalist relationships have clear boundaries. It's about knowing when to say no, setting limits on your time and energy, and prioritizing your well-being.

Benefits of Minimalist Relationships

Embracing minimalist principles in your relationships can offer a wide range of benefits:

1. **Deeper Connections**: By focusing on quality over quantity, minimalist relationships allow for deeper, more meaningful connections with others.
2. **Less Drama**: Minimalist relationships are free from the drama and stress that often accompany complex or superficial relationships.
3. **More Time and Energy**: By decluttering your social life, you free up time and energy to invest in the relationships that truly matter to you.
4. **Improved Well-being**: Meaningful connections are essential for our emotional and mental well-being. Minimalist relationships can lead to greater happiness and fulfillment.

5. **Greater Focus**: By simplifying your relationships, you can focus on what truly matters, whether it's your family, close friends, or partner.

Practical Tips for Cultivating Minimalist Relationships

1. **Declutter Your Social Circle**: Take inventory of your relationships and consider which ones bring value to your life and which ones may be draining or unfulfilling. Focus your time and energy on those that matter most to you.
2. **Set Boundaries**: Establish clear boundaries in your relationships to protect your time, energy, and well-being. Learn to say no to activities or people that don't align with your values or priorities.
3. **Practice Active Listening**: Truly listen to others when they speak, without distractions or interruptions. Show empathy and understanding in your interactions.
4. **Spend Quality Time Together**: Instead of spreading yourself thin with numerous social commitments, prioritize spending quality time with loved ones. Focus on creating meaningful memories together.
5. **Communicate Openly and Honestly**: Be transparent in your communication with others. Share your thoughts, feelings, and needs openly, and encourage others to do the same.

Minimalism in relationships is about cultivating meaningful connections, decluttering your social life, and focusing on what truly matters. By embracing minimalist principles in your relationships, you can deepen your connections with others, reduce stress and drama, and create a more fulfilling and intentional social life. Remember, it's not about the quantity of relationships you have, but the quality of those relationships that truly matters.

12.FINDING BALANCE

Work, Life, and Minimalism

In our fast-paced and often overwhelming world, finding balance between work and life can be a daunting challenge. The pressures of modern life can leave us feeling stressed, exhausted, and disconnected from what truly matters. However, by embracing minimalist principles, we can create a more harmonious and fulfilling life that prioritizes what is truly important. This article will explore the concept of finding balance through minimalism, offer practical tips for achieving work-life balance, and provide guidance on how to live a more intentional and meaningful life.

Understanding Work-Life Balance

Work-life balance is about more than just dividing your time between work and personal activities. It's about finding harmony between the various aspects of your life, including work, family, health, and personal interests. It's about prioritizing what is truly important to you and creating boundaries that allow you to focus on those priorities.

The Role of Minimalism in Finding Balance

Minimalism can play a key role in helping you find balance in your life. By simplifying your life and focusing on what truly matters, you can reduce the distractions and stressors that can interfere with achieving balance. Minimalism encourages you to:

1. **Prioritize Your Values**: Minimalism encourages you to identify your core values and prioritize them in your life. By focusing on what truly matters to you, you can make decisions that align with your values and bring you fulfillment.
2. **Eliminate Excess**: Minimalism encourages you to eliminate excess possessions, commitments, and distractions that can clutter your life and prevent you from finding balance.
3. **Create Space for What Matters**: By simplifying your life, you create space for the things that truly matter to you, whether it's spending time with loved ones, pursuing a passion, or taking care of your health.
4. **Reduce Stress**: Minimalism can help reduce the stress and overwhelm that can come from juggling too many commitments and possessions. By simplifying your life, you can create a more peaceful and harmonious environment.

Practical Tips for Finding Balance Through Minimalism

1. **Set Priorities**: Identify your core values and priorities, and use them to guide your decisions about how to spend your time and energy.
2. **Create Boundaries**: Set boundaries between work and personal life to ensure that you have time for both. This may involve

setting specific work hours, limiting work-related activities outside of those hours, and prioritizing personal time for relaxation and rejuvenation.

3. **Simplify Your Schedule**: Avoid over-scheduling yourself and learn to say no to commitments that do not align with your priorities.

4. **Declutter Your Space**: Simplify your physical environment by decluttering your home and workspace. A clutter-free environment can help reduce stress and create a sense of calm.

5. **Practice Mindfulness**: Be present in the moment and pay attention to your thoughts, feelings, and physical sensations. Mindfulness can help you stay focused on what truly matters and avoid getting caught up in distractions.

Finding balance in today's hectic world is a constant challenge, but by embracing minimalist principles, you can create a more harmonious and fulfilling life. By prioritizing your values, simplifying your life, and creating space for what matters most, you can achieve a greater sense of balance and well-being. Embrace minimalism as a tool to help you find the balance you seek, and enjoy a more intentional and meaningful life.

13.MINIMALIST MINDSET

Shifting Your Perspective

I n a world that often equates success and happiness with the accumulation of wealth, possessions, and accomplishments, adopting a minimalist mindset can seem counterintuitive. However, at its core, minimalism is not just about decluttering your physical space; it's about shifting your perspective and reevaluating your priorities. By embracing a minimalist mindset, you can cultivate a more intentional and fulfilling life that focuses on what truly matters. This article will explore the concept of a minimalist mindset, offer practical tips for adopting one, and provide guidance on how to shift your perspective to embrace simplicity and contentment.

Understanding the Minimalist Mindset

At its essence, a minimalist mindset is about questioning the status quo and challenging conventional notions of success and happiness. It's about recognizing that true fulfillment does not come from the accumulation of material possessions or the pursuit of external validation, but from within. A minimalist mindset is characterized by several key principles:

1. **Intentionality**: A minimalist mindset is guided by intentionality in all areas of life. It involves being deliberate and purposeful in your actions, choices, and priorities.
2. **Simplicity**: A minimalist mindset embraces simplicity in all aspects of life, from the possessions you own to the way you spend your time and energy.
3. **Gratitude**: A minimalist mindset cultivates a sense of gratitude for what you have, rather than focusing on what you lack. It involves appreciating the abundance that exists in your life, regardless of material wealth.
4. **Mindfulness**: A minimalist mindset encourages mindfulness, or the practice of being present in the moment and aware of your thoughts, feelings, and surroundings.
5. **Contentment**: A minimalist mindset is rooted in contentment, or the ability to find satisfaction and joy in the present moment, rather than constantly striving for more.

Benefits of Adopting a Minimalist Mindset

Embracing a minimalist mindset offers numerous benefits that can positively impact your life:

1. **Increased Clarity**: A minimalist mindset can help you clarify your values, priorities, and goals, allowing you to make decisions that align with what truly matters to you.
2. **Reduced Stress**: By simplifying your life and focusing on what's important, you can reduce stress and overwhelm, leading to greater peace of mind.
3. **Improved Relationships**: A minimalist mindset can improve your relationships by encouraging deeper connections and more meaningful interactions with others.

4. **Enhanced Creativity**: Simplifying your life can free up mental space and energy, allowing for greater creativity and innovation.
5. **Environmental Impact**: Adopting a minimalist mindset can reduce your environmental impact by encouraging conscious consumption and reducing waste.

Practical Tips for Adopting a Minimalist Mindset

1. **Reflect on Your Values**: Take time to reflect on your values and priorities, and consider how they align with your current lifestyle.
2. **Declutter Your Space**: Start by decluttering your physical space, removing items that no longer serve a purpose or bring you joy.
3. **Simplify Your Schedule**: Evaluate your commitments and activities, and prioritize those that align with your values and goals.
4. **Practice Gratitude**: Cultivate a daily gratitude practice to focus on the positive aspects of your life and appreciate what you have.
5. **Focus on Experiences Over Possessions**: Instead of focusing on acquiring more possessions, prioritize experiences that bring you joy and fulfilment.

Adopting a minimalist mindset is not about depriving yourself or living a life of austerity. It's about embracing simplicity, intentionality, and contentment in all areas of your life. By shifting your perspective and re-evaluating your priorities, you can cultivate a more intentional and fulfilling life that is aligned with your values and goals. Embrace the minimalist mindset as a tool to help you find clarity, reduce stress, and create a life that is rich in meaning and purpose.

14.THE ENVIRONMENTAL IMPACT OF MINIMALISM

Living Sustainably

In a world facing increasing environmental challenges, the concept of minimalism has gained traction as a lifestyle choice that promotes sustainability and reduces waste. Minimalism is not just about decluttering your physical space; it's about reevaluating your consumption habits, prioritizing quality over quantity, and living more intentionally. By embracing minimalist principles, you can not only simplify your life but also reduce your environmental impact and contribute to a more sustainable future. This article will explore the environmental impact of minimalism, offer practical tips for living sustainably, and provide guidance on how to incorporate minimalist principles into your daily life.

Understanding the Environmental Impact of Minimalism

Minimalism has several environmental benefits that stem from its core principles:

1. **Reduced Consumption**: Minimalism encourages you to buy less and make more mindful purchasing decisions. By reducing your consumption, you can reduce the demand for new products, which in turn reduces the environmental impact of manufacturing and transportation.
2. **Less Waste**: Minimalism advocates for decluttering and owning fewer possessions. This leads to less waste being generated, as you are less likely to throw away items that you no longer need or use.
3. **Energy Conservation**: Owning fewer possessions means using less energy for production, transportation, and storage. This can help reduce greenhouse gas emissions and lessen your carbon footprint.
4. **Support for Sustainable Practices**: By prioritizing quality over quantity, minimalism encourages you to support companies and products that prioritize sustainability and ethical practices.

Practical Tips for Living Sustainably Through Minimalism

1. **Declutter Responsibly**: When decluttering, consider donating or selling items that are in good condition instead of throwing them away. This reduces waste and allows others to benefit from your unwanted items.
2. **Buy Secondhand**: Instead of buying new, consider purchasing secondhand items. This reduces the demand for new products and extends the life of existing ones.
3. **Choose Quality Over Quantity**: Invest in high-quality, durable items that will last longer and reduce the need for frequent replacements.
4. **Reduce Single-Use Items**: Minimize the use of single-use items such as plastic bags, bottles, and utensils. Instead, opt for

reusable alternatives.

5. **Conserve Energy**: Practice energy conservation by turning off lights and appliances when not in use, using energy-efficient appliances, and reducing heating and cooling costs through insulation and temperature control.

6. **Support Sustainable Brands**: Research and support brands that prioritize sustainability, ethical sourcing, and environmentally friendly practices.

The Role of Minimalism in Environmental Conservation

Minimalism is not a one-size-fits-all solution to environmental issues, but it can be a powerful tool for reducing waste and promoting sustainability. By adopting a minimalist lifestyle, you can reduce your environmental impact, conserve resources, and contribute to a more sustainable future for our planet. Embrace minimalism as a mindset that values quality over quantity, mindfulness over consumerism, and sustainability over excess. Together, we can create a more sustainable world for future generations.

15.TRAVELING LIGHT

Minimalist Travel Tips

Traveling can be an exciting and enriching experience, but it can also be stressful and overwhelming, especially if you're weighed down by excessive luggage and belongings. Adopting a minimalist approach to travel can help you streamline your packing, reduce stress, and enhance your overall travel experience. In this article, we'll explore the concept of minimalist travel, offer practical tips for traveling light, and provide guidance on how to make the most of your minimalist travel adventure.

Understanding Minimalist Travel

Minimalist travel is about more than just packing light; it's about adopting a mindset that prioritizes experiences over possessions and values simplicity and efficiency in your travel habits. Minimalist travel involves:

1. **Packing Light**: Traveling with only the essentials and avoiding unnecessary items that add bulk to your luggage.

2. **Simplifying Your Itinerary**: Focusing on a few key destinations or experiences rather than trying to see and do everything.
3. **Embracing Spontaneity**: Allowing for flexibility in your plans and being open to unexpected opportunities and experiences.
4. **Prioritizing Experiences**: Choosing activities and experiences that align with your interests and values, rather than following a prescribed tourist itinerary.
5. **Mindful Consumption**: Being mindful of the impact your travel habits have on the environment and local communities, and striving to minimize negative impacts.

Benefits of Minimalist Travel

Embracing minimalist travel offers a range of benefits that can enhance your travel experience:

1. **Reduced Stress**: Traveling light can reduce the stress of lugging heavy luggage and simplify your travel experience.
2. **Increased Freedom**: Traveling with less allows for greater flexibility and spontaneity in your travels.
3. **Cost Savings**: Traveling light can save you money on baggage fees and transportation costs.
4. **Environmental Impact**: Minimalist travel can reduce your environmental impact by minimizing waste and carbon emissions associated with excess luggage.
5. **Enhanced Experience**: By focusing on experiences over possessions, minimalist travel can lead to more meaningful and memorable travel experiences.

Practical Tips for Minimalist Travel

1. **Pack Light**: Choose versatile, multi-purpose clothing and limit yourself to essentials. Consider using a smaller, carry-on sized suitcase or backpack.
2. **Plan Ahead**: Research your destination and pack accordingly. Consider the weather, local customs, and activities you plan to

participate in.

3. **Use Technology**: Instead of carrying physical books or maps, use digital resources like e-books and maps apps on your smartphone or tablet.
4. **Limit Electronics**: Consider leaving unnecessary electronics at home or opting for multi-functional devices like a smartphone or tablet.
5. **Embrace Slow Travel**: Instead of trying to see and do everything, focus on a few key experiences and take the time to truly immerse yourself in the local culture.

Minimalist travel is not about sacrificing comfort or missing out on experiences; it's about enhancing your travel experience by focusing on what truly matters and eliminating unnecessary distractions. By adopting a minimalist approach to travel, you can reduce stress, save money, and make the most of your travel adventures. So, pack light, travel smart, and embrace the freedom and flexibility that minimalist travel has to offer.

16.MINIMALIST WELLNESS

Simplifying Your Health Routine

In today's fast-paced world, maintaining our health and well-being can often feel like an overwhelming task. We are bombarded with messages about the latest health trends, superfoods, and fitness routines, leading many of us to believe that achieving optimal health requires a complex and time-consuming approach. However, embracing a minimalist approach to wellness can offer a refreshing perspective, showing us that simplicity and balance are key to achieving lasting health and vitality. This article will explore the concept of minimalist wellness, offer practical tips for simplifying your health routine, and provide guidance on how to prioritize your well-being in a hectic world.

Understanding Minimalist Wellness

Minimalist wellness is about more than just following a strict diet or exercise regimen; it's about adopting a holistic approach to health that focuses on simplicity, balance, and sustainability. At its core, minimalist wellness is guided by several key principles:

1. **Simplicity**: Minimalist wellness emphasizes simplicity in all aspects of health, from diet and exercise to self-care and stress management. It involves stripping away unnecessary complexity and focusing on the essentials.
2. **Balance**: Minimalist wellness encourages balance in all areas of life, recognizing that health is not just about physical well-being, but also mental, emotional, and spiritual well-being.
3. **Mindfulness**: Minimalist wellness involves practicing mindfulness in your health routine, paying attention to your body's signals and making choices that support your overall well-being.
4. **Sustainability**: Minimalist wellness emphasizes sustainable practices that promote long-term health and well-being, rather than quick fixes or fad diets.
5. **Self-Care**: Minimalist wellness prioritizes self-care and self-compassion, recognizing that taking care of yourself is essential for maintaining health and vitality.

The Benefits of Minimalist Wellness

Embracing minimalist wellness offers numerous benefits that can positively impact your life:

1. **Improved Health**: By simplifying your health routine and focusing on the essentials, you can improve your overall health and well-being.
2. **Reduced Stress**: Minimalist wellness can help reduce stress and overwhelm by simplifying your approach to health and prioritizing self-care.
3. **Increased Energy**: By adopting a balanced and sustainable health routine, you can increase your energy levels and improve

your overall quality of life.

4. **Enhanced Mental Clarity**: Minimalist wellness can help improve mental clarity and focus, allowing you to be more present and engaged in your daily life.
5. **Better Relationships**: Taking care of your health and well-being can improve your relationships with others, as you will have more energy and positivity to share.

Practical Tips for Minimalist Wellness

1. **Simplify Your Diet**: Focus on whole, unprocessed foods and listen to your body's hunger and fullness cues. Avoid restrictive diets and instead aim for balance and moderation.
2. **Prioritize Sleep**: Ensure you get enough restful sleep each night by establishing a regular bedtime routine and creating a comfortable sleep environment.
3. **Move Your Body**: Find enjoyable ways to move your body regularly, whether it's through walking, yoga, or other forms of exercise. Focus on activities that you love and that make you feel good.
4. **Practice Mindfulness**: Incorporate mindfulness practices into your daily routine, such as meditation, deep breathing, or journaling. These practices can help reduce stress and improve mental clarity.
5. **Simplify Your Self-Care Routine**: Identify the self-care practices that truly nourish you and incorporate them into your daily life. This could include things like taking a relaxing bath, spending time in nature, or practicing gratitude.

Minimalist wellness offers a simple yet powerful approach to health and well-being, emphasizing balance, simplicity, and sustainability. By adopting a minimalist mindset and simplifying your health routine, you can achieve lasting health and vitality while reducing stress and overwhelm.

Embrace minimalist wellness as a guiding principle in your life, and discover the transformative power of simplicity in achieving optimal health and well-being.

17.MINIMALISM AND CREATIVITY

Embracing Simplicity in Art and Innovation

I n the world of art and innovation, the concept of minimalism has long been revered for its ability to strip away the unnecessary and reveal the essential. From visual arts to music, architecture to technology, minimalism has influenced countless creators and innovators, inspiring them to embrace simplicity and focus on what truly matters. This article explores the relationship between minimalism and creativity, highlighting how the principles of minimalism can enhance artistic expression and drive innovation.

Understanding Minimalism in Art and Innovation

Minimalism is more than just a visual style; it's a mindset that prioritizes simplicity, clarity, and intentionality. In art, minimalism often involves the use of simple forms, monochromatic color palettes, and a focus on space and proportion. In innovation, minimalism is about finding elegant solutions to complex problems, stripping away unnecessary features and focusing on the core functionality.

At its core, minimalism is about distilling ideas down to their essence, removing distractions, and allowing the true beauty and power of an idea to shine through. This approach can lead to more impactful and meaningful artistic creations, as well as more efficient and effective innovations.

The Influence of Minimalism on Art

Minimalism has had a profound influence on the world of art, shaping the work of countless artists across various mediums. In visual arts, artists like Donald Judd, Agnes Martin, and Dan Flavin embraced minimalism, creating works that emphasized simplicity, geometry, and repetition.

In music, composers like Philip Glass and Steve Reich explored minimalist techniques, using repetition and gradual change to create mesmerizing compositions. In literature, writers like Ernest Hemingway and Raymond Carver embraced minimalism, using sparse language and understated prose to convey powerful emotions.

The Impact of Minimalism on Innovation

Innovation is another area where minimalism has had a significant impact. In product design, companies like Apple have embraced minimalism, creating products that are not only visually appealing but also intuitive and user-friendly.

In technology, minimalist design principles have led to the development of sleek, efficient, and user-friendly interfaces that prioritize functionality over complexity. In architecture, minimalist principles have influenced the design of buildings that are not only beautiful but also efficient and sustainable.

Practical Tips for Embracing Minimalism in Creativity

1. **Focus on the Essential**: Identify the core idea or message you want to convey and strip away anything that distracts from it.
2. **Simplify Your Process**: Streamline your creative process by eliminating unnecessary steps and focusing on the most effective techniques.
3. **Embrace Constraints**: Use limitations as a creative challenge, forcing you to find innovative solutions within a set of constraints.
4. **Create Space for Creativity**: Clear your physical and mental space of clutter to allow for more focused and inspired creative work.
5. **Iterate and Refine**: Continuously refine your work, removing anything that doesn't contribute to the overall impact or effectiveness of your creation.

Minimalism offers a powerful framework for enhancing creativity and driving innovation. By embracing simplicity, clarity, and intentionality in our artistic and innovative pursuits, we can create work that is not only visually striking and innovative but also meaningful and impactful.

Whether you're an artist, a designer, an innovator, or simply someone looking to enhance your creativity, embracing the principles of minimalism can help you unlock new levels of artistic expression and innovation.

18. THE MINIMALIST ENTREPRENEUR

Building a Business with Purpose

In a world where entrepreneurship is often equated with hustle culture and the relentless pursuit of growth, adopting a minimalist approach to business can offer a refreshing alternative. Minimalist entrepreneurs prioritize simplicity, intentionality, and purpose in their business practices, focusing on what truly matters and eliminating distractions. This article explores the concept of the minimalist entrepreneur, offering insights into how to build a successful business with purpose and meaning.

Understanding Minimalist Entrepreneurship

Minimalist entrepreneurship is about more than just running a lean business; it's about aligning your business practices with your values and priorities. Minimalist entrepreneurs prioritize:

1. **Simplicity**: Minimalist entrepreneurs simplify their business practices, focusing on the essentials and eliminating unnecessary complexity.
2. **Intentionality**: Minimalist entrepreneurs are intentional about their business decisions, ensuring that each action aligns with their overall goals and values.
3. **Purpose**: Minimalist entrepreneurs prioritize purpose over profit, seeking to create meaningful impact through their business endeavors.
4. **Sustainability**: Minimalist entrepreneurs focus on building sustainable businesses that can thrive in the long term, rather than pursuing short-term gains at the expense of the environment or society.

The Benefits of Minimalist Entrepreneurship

Embracing a minimalist approach to entrepreneurship offers numerous benefits:

1. **Clarity of Purpose**: By simplifying their business practices, minimalist entrepreneurs gain clarity of purpose, allowing them to focus on what truly matters.
2. **Efficiency**: Minimalist entrepreneurs eliminate waste and inefficiency in their business processes, leading to greater productivity and profitability.
3. **Resilience**: Minimalist businesses are often more resilient to economic downturns and market fluctuations, as they are not overly reliant on external factors for success.
4. **Positive Impact**: Minimalist entrepreneurs prioritize creating positive impact through their business endeavors, leading to greater fulfillment and satisfaction.

Practical Tips for Minimalist Entrepreneurship

1. **Focus on Your Core Offering**: Identify your core product or service and focus on delivering it exceptionally well, rather than

trying to offer a wide range of products or services.

2. **Streamline Your Operations**: Simplify your business processes and eliminate any steps that do not add value to your customers or your business.

3. **Embrace Digital Tools**: Use digital tools and technology to streamline your business operations and reduce the need for physical resources.

4. **Build a Strong Brand**: Focus on building a strong brand that resonates with your target audience and reflects your values and priorities.

5. **Practice Conscious Consumption**: Be mindful of the resources you consume in your business operations, and seek to minimize waste and environmental impact.

Minimalist entrepreneurship offers a compelling approach to building a business with purpose and meaning. By simplifying your business practices, focusing on what truly matters, and prioritizing sustainability and positive impact, you can create a business that not only generates profit but also contributes to a better world. Embrace the principles of minimalist entrepreneurship, and discover the power of building a business with purpose and intentionality.

19.MINIMALIST LEISURE

Finding Joy in Simple Pleasures

I n today's fast-paced world, our leisure time is often filled with distractions and busyness, leaving us feeling drained and unfulfilled. However, by embracing a minimalist approach to leisure, we can rediscover the joy of simple pleasures and create more meaningful experiences in our lives. This article will explore the concept of minimalist leisure, offer practical tips for simplifying your leisure time, and provide guidance on how to find joy in the simple pleasures of life.

Understanding Minimalist Leisure

Minimalist leisure is about more than just cutting back on activities or decluttering your schedule; it's about intentionally choosing how you spend your leisure time and prioritizing activities that bring you true joy and fulfillment. At its core, minimalist leisure is guided by several key principles:

1. **Simplicity**: Minimalist leisure emphasizes simplicity in all aspects of your leisure activities, from the activities themselves to the way you approach them. It involves stripping away the unnecessary and focusing on what truly brings you joy.
2. **Presence**: Minimalist leisure encourages being present in the moment and fully engaging in your leisure activities. It's about savoring the experience and being mindful of the beauty and joy that surrounds you.
3. **Mindfulness**: Minimalist leisure involves being mindful of how you spend your leisure time and making intentional choices that align with your values and priorities.
4. **Quality Over Quantity**: Minimalist leisure prioritizes quality over quantity, focusing on meaningful experiences rather than the quantity of activities.
5. **Gratitude**: Minimalist leisure involves cultivating a sense of gratitude for the simple pleasures of life and appreciating the beauty and joy that surrounds you.

Benefits of Minimalist Leisure

Embracing minimalist leisure offers numerous benefits that can positively impact your life:

1. **Increased Joy**: By focusing on activities that bring you true joy and fulfillment, minimalist leisure can enhance your overall sense of well-being and happiness.
2. **Reduced Stress**: Minimalist leisure can help reduce stress and overwhelm by simplifying your leisure activities and allowing you to relax and recharge.
3. **Improved Relationships**: Spending quality time with loved ones and engaging in meaningful leisure activities can strengthen your relationships and deepen your connections with others.
4. **Enhanced Creativity**: Simplifying your leisure activities can free up mental space and energy, allowing for greater creativity and inspiration.

5. **Greater Appreciation for Life**: By focusing on the simple pleasures of life, minimalist leisure can help you develop a greater appreciation for the beauty and joy that surrounds you.

Practical Tips for Minimalist Leisure

1. **Simplify Your Schedule**: Avoid over-scheduling yourself and leave room for spontaneous leisure activities.
2. **Focus on One Thing at a Time**: Practice single-tasking during your leisure time, fully immersing yourself in the activity at hand.
3. **Disconnect from Technology**: Take regular breaks from screens and digital devices to fully engage in the present moment.
4. **Spend Time in Nature**: Nature has a calming and rejuvenating effect, so try to spend time outdoors whenever possible.
5. **Practice Gratitude**: Take time to appreciate the simple pleasures of life, such as a beautiful sunset or a warm cup of tea.

Minimalist leisure offers a refreshing perspective on how to find joy and fulfilment in your leisure time. By simplifying your leisure activities and focusing on what truly brings you joy, you can create more meaningful experiences and cultivate a greater appreciation for the simple pleasures of life. Embrace minimalist leisure as a guiding principle in your life, and discover the joy and fulfilment that comes from finding joy in the simple pleasures of life.

20.MINIMALISM IN A DIGITAL WORLD

Navigating Social Media and Technology

I n today's digital age, our lives are more connected than ever before. We rely on technology for communication, information, and entertainment, often spending hours each day interacting with screens. While technology has undoubtedly improved many aspects of our lives, it has also brought with it a host of challenges, including digital clutter, information overload, and the constant distraction of social media. Minimalism offers a refreshing perspective on how to navigate the digital world with intentionality and purpose. This article will explore the concept of minimalism in a digital world, offer practical tips for simplifying your digital life, and provide guidance on how to find balance in an increasingly connected world.

Understanding Minimalism in a Digital World

Minimalism in a digital world is about more than just decluttering your digital devices; it's about being intentional and mindful about how you use technology. It's about recognizing the impact that technology can have on your mental health, productivity, and overall well-being, and making conscious choices to minimize its negative effects. At its core, minimalism in a digital world is guided by several key principles:

1. **Digital Decluttering**: Minimalism in a digital world involves decluttering your digital devices and online accounts, removing unnecessary apps, files, and subscriptions.
2. **Mindful Consumption**: Minimalism in a digital world encourages mindful consumption of digital content, avoiding the trap of endless scrolling and information overload.
3. **Intentional Use**: Minimalism in a digital world emphasizes intentional use of technology, using it as a tool to enhance your life rather than as a source of constant distraction.
4. **Digital Detox**: Minimalism in a digital world includes regular digital detoxes, taking breaks from screens to recharge and reconnect with the world around you.
5. **Balanced Approach**: Minimalism in a digital world promotes a balanced approach to technology, finding a healthy balance between digital and offline activities.

The Impact of Technology on Mental Health

Technology has revolutionized the way we communicate, work, and socialize, but it has also had a profound impact on our mental health. Excessive use of social media has been linked to feelings of loneliness, anxiety, and depression, while constant connectivity can lead to burnout and overwhelm. By adopting a minimalist approach to technology, we can mitigate these negative effects and create a healthier relationship with our digital devices.

Practical Tips for Minimalism in a Digital World

1. **Digital Decluttering**: Regularly declutter your digital devices and online accounts, removing apps, files, and subscriptions that no longer serve a purpose.
2. **Set Boundaries**: Establish boundaries around your technology use, such as limiting screen time or designating tech-free zones in your home.
3. **Practice Mindful Consumption**: Be mindful of the content you consume online, avoiding mindless scrolling and focusing on content that enriches your life.
4. **Take Digital Breaks**: Schedule regular breaks from screens to recharge and engage in offline activities.
5. **Prioritize Quality Over Quantity**: Focus on quality interactions and experiences online, rather than seeking validation through likes and comments.

Minimalism in a digital world offers a powerful framework for navigating the complexities of our digital age. By adopting a minimalist approach to technology, we can simplify our digital lives, reduce stress and overwhelm, and find greater balance and fulfilment in an increasingly connected world. Embrace minimalism as a guiding principle in your digital life, and discover the joy and freedom that comes from living with intentionality and purpose in a digital world.

21.MINIMALIST SELF-CARE

Prioritizing Your Well-being

I n a world that often glorifies busyness and productivity, self-care is often overlooked or seen as indulgent. However, self-care is an essential component of maintaining overall health and well-being. It is about taking the time to prioritize your physical, mental, and emotional needs in order to prevent burnout and improve your quality of life. Minimalist self-care takes this concept a step further by encouraging a simplified approach to self-care that focuses on the essentials and avoids unnecessary complexity. This article will explore the concept of minimalist self-care, offer practical tips for incorporating minimalist self-care into your life, and provide guidance on how to prioritize your well-being in a hectic world.

Understanding Minimalist Self-Care

Minimalist self-care is about more than just bubble baths and face masks; it's about taking a holistic approach to caring for yourself that is simple, intentional, and sustainable. At its core, minimalist self-care is guided by several key principles:

1. **Simplicity**: Minimalist self-care emphasizes simplicity in all aspects of self-care, from the activities themselves to the way you approach them. It involves focusing on the essentials and avoiding unnecessary complexity.
2. **Intentionality**: Minimalist self-care encourages being intentional about how you care for yourself, choosing activities that truly nourish and rejuvenate you.
3. **Consistency**: Minimalist self-care involves making self-care a regular part of your routine, rather than something you only do occasionally.
4. **Self-Compassion**: Minimalist self-care emphasizes self-compassion and self-acceptance, recognizing that caring for yourself is essential for overall well-being.
5. **Balance**: Minimalist self-care promotes a balanced approach to self-care, recognizing that self-care is not just about pampering yourself, but also about taking care of your physical, mental, and emotional health.

The Importance of Minimalist Self-Care

Self-care is often viewed as a luxury or something that is only necessary when you are feeling overwhelmed or stressed. However, self-care is an essential part of maintaining your overall health and well-being. When you prioritize self-care, you are better able to manage stress, prevent burnout, and improve your overall quality of life. Minimalist self-care offers a simple and sustainable approach to self-care that can be easily incorporated into your daily routine.

Practical Tips for Minimalist Self-Care

1. **Establish a Routine**: Create a regular self-care routine that includes activities that nourish your body, mind, and spirit.
2. **Simplify Your Environment**: Declutter your physical space to create a peaceful and calming environment that supports your well-being.
3. **Practice Mindfulness**: Incorporate mindfulness practices into your daily routine, such as meditation, yoga, or deep breathing exercises.
4. **Connect with Nature**: Spend time outdoors and connect with the natural world to rejuvenate your mind and body.
5. **Prioritize Sleep**: Ensure you get enough restful sleep each night by establishing a regular bedtime routine and creating a comfortable sleep environment.

Minimalist self-care is a powerful tool for improving your overall health and well-being. By simplifying your approach to self-care and focusing on the essentials, you can create a more sustainable and fulfilling self-care routine that supports your physical, mental, and emotional health. Embrace minimalist self-care as a guiding principle in your life, and discover the joy and freedom that comes from prioritizing your well-being in a hectic world.

22.MINIMALIST GARDENING

Creating a Tranquil Outdoor Space

In the hustle and bustle of modern life, our outdoor spaces can serve as sanctuaries of tranquility and beauty. Minimalist gardening offers a unique approach to creating outdoor spaces that are not only visually appealing but also easy to maintain and conducive to relaxation. This article will explore the concept of minimalist gardening, offer practical tips for creating a minimalist garden, and provide guidance on how to cultivate a tranquil outdoor space that enhances your minimalist lifestyle.

Understanding Minimalist Gardening

Minimalist gardening is about more than just having a tidy garden; it's about creating a harmonious and balanced outdoor space that complements your minimalist lifestyle.

At its core, minimalist gardening is guided by several key principles:

1. **Simplicity**: Minimalist gardening emphasizes simplicity in design and maintenance, focusing on clean lines, uncluttered spaces, and a limited color palette.
2. **Functionality**: Minimalist gardening prioritizes functionality, with a focus on creating outdoor spaces that are both beautiful and practical.
3. **Natural Materials**: Minimalist gardening often incorporates natural materials, such as stone, wood, and gravel, to create a sense of harmony with the surrounding environment.
4. **Sustainable Practices**: Minimalist gardening embraces sustainable practices, such as composting, rainwater harvesting, and using native plants, to minimize environmental impact.
5. **Mindfulness**: Minimalist gardening encourages mindfulness in your garden activities, encouraging you to be present in the moment and enjoy the process of gardening.

Creating a Minimalist Garden

Creating a minimalist garden doesn't have to be complicated. By following a few simple guidelines, you can create a tranquil outdoor space that reflects your minimalist lifestyle:

1. **Start with a Plan**: Before you begin, take some time to plan your garden layout and design. Consider the size and shape of your space, as well as the types of plants and materials you want to use.
2. **Focus on Quality Over Quantity**: Instead of filling your garden with a wide variety of plants and decorations, focus on a few key elements that will make a big impact.

3. **Use Natural Materials**: Incorporate natural materials, such as stone, wood, and gravel, into your garden design to create a cohesive and harmonious look.
4. **Choose Low-Maintenance Plants**: Select plants that are easy to care for and require minimal watering and pruning. Native plants are often a good choice, as they are well-suited to your local climate and soil conditions.
5. **Create Restful Spaces**: Include areas in your garden where you can relax and unwind, such as a seating area or a quiet corner with a bench or hammock.

Maintaining a Minimalist Garden

Once your minimalist garden is in place, maintaining it is relatively simple. Regular maintenance tasks, such as weeding, pruning, and watering, will help keep your garden looking its best. Additionally, periodic assessments of your garden's design and layout can help you identify any areas that may need adjustment or improvement.

Minimalist gardening offers a unique approach to creating outdoor spaces that are not only beautiful but also easy to maintain and conducive to relaxation. By following the principles of simplicity, functionality, and sustainability, you can create a tranquil outdoor space that enhances your minimalist lifestyle. Embrace minimalist gardening as a way to connect with nature, cultivate mindfulness, and create a peaceful oasis in your own backyard.

23.MINIMALIST HOLIDAYS

Simplifying the Festive Season

The holiday season is often a time of joy and celebration, but it can also be a time of stress and overwhelm. The pressure to buy gifts, decorate the house, and attend numerous gatherings can leave us feeling exhausted and drained. However, by embracing a minimalist approach to the holidays, we can simplify the festive season and focus on what truly matters. This article will explore the concept of minimalist holidays, offer practical tips for simplifying your holiday celebrations, and provide guidance on how to find joy and meaning in the season.

Understanding Minimalist Holidays

Minimalist holidays are about more than just cutting back on decorations or gifts; they're about rethinking the way we approach the holiday season as a whole. At its core, minimalist holidays are guided by several key principles:

1. **Simplicity**: Minimalist holidays emphasize simplicity in all aspects of the season, from decorations and gifts to activities and gatherings. It's about focusing on quality over quantity and avoiding the excess that can often accompany the holidays.
2. **Mindful Consumption**: Minimalist holidays encourage mindful consumption, encouraging us to think carefully about the gifts we give and receive, as well as the food we eat and the decorations we use.
3. **Meaningful Connections**: Minimalist holidays prioritize meaningful connections with loved ones, focusing on spending quality time together rather than getting caught up in the busyness of the season.
4. **Gratitude**: Minimalist holidays cultivate a sense of gratitude for the simple pleasures of the season, such as cozy evenings by the fire or a warm cup of cocoa with loved ones.
5. **Creating Traditions**: Minimalist holidays involve creating meaningful traditions that can be enjoyed year after year, focusing on experiences rather than material possessions.

Practical Tips for Minimalist Holidays

1. **Simplify Decorations**: Instead of elaborate decorations, opt for simple, natural elements like greenery, candles, and pinecones.
2. **Mindful Gift Giving**: Focus on giving gifts that are meaningful and thoughtful, rather than expensive or extravagant. Consider giving experiences or homemade gifts rather than material items.
3. **Limit Social Obligations**: Be selective about the gatherings and events you attend, prioritizing those that are most important to you and your loved ones.
4. **Focus on Experiences**: Instead of focusing on material gifts, create experiences that you can enjoy together, such as a holiday movie night or a walk in the snow.
5. **Practice Self-Care**: Take time to care for yourself during the busy holiday season, whether it's through meditation, exercise, or simply taking a few moments to relax and unwind.

Minimalist holidays offer a refreshing perspective on the festive season, emphasizing simplicity, mindfulness, and meaningful connections. By embracing the principles of minimalism, we can simplify our holiday celebrations and focus on what truly matters, creating a season that is both joyful and meaningful. Embrace minimalist holidays as a way to reduce stress, create lasting memories, and find true joy in the season.

24.MINIMALIST PHILANTHROPY

Giving Back with Purpose

In a world filled with complexity and clutter, the concept of minimalist philanthropy offers a refreshing approach to giving back. Minimalist philanthropy is not just about writing a check or donating items; it's about giving with intentionality and purpose, focusing on making a meaningful impact rather than simply giving for the sake of giving. This article will explore the concept of minimalist philanthropy, offer practical tips for giving back with purpose, and provide guidance on how to make a meaningful difference in the world.

Understanding Minimalist Philanthropy

Minimalist philanthropy is rooted in the principles of minimalism, which emphasize simplicity, intentionality, and mindfulness. At its core, minimalist philanthropy is guided by several key principles:

1. **Purposeful Giving**: Minimalist philanthropy involves giving with a clear purpose and goal in mind, focusing on making a meaningful impact in a specific area or community.
2. **Sustainable Impact**: Minimalist philanthropy prioritizes sustainable impact, looking for ways to create lasting change rather than providing temporary solutions.
3. **Mindful Consumption**: Minimalist philanthropy encourages mindful consumption, recognizing the impact that our purchasing decisions can have on others and the environment.
4. **Transparency and Accountability**: Minimalist philanthropy values transparency and accountability, ensuring that donations are used effectively and responsibly.
5. **Personal Engagement**: Minimalist philanthropy emphasizes personal engagement, encouraging donors to be actively involved in the causes they support.

Practical Tips for Minimalist Philanthropy

1. **Identify Your Values**: Start by identifying the causes and issues that are most important to you. This will help you focus your philanthropic efforts and make a greater impact.
2. **Research Organizations**: Take the time to research organizations that align with your values and have a track record of making a meaningful impact in their field.
3. **Give Strategically**: Instead of spreading your donations thin, consider focusing your giving on a few key organizations or causes where you can make a significant impact.
4. **Volunteer Your Time**: In addition to financial contributions, consider volunteering your time and skills to organizations that could benefit from your expertise.
5. **Spread Awareness**: Use your voice and platform to raise awareness about the causes you care about, helping to educate others and inspire action.

Minimalist philanthropy offers a powerful way to give back with purpose and intentionality. By embracing the principles of minimalist philanthropy, we can make a meaningful impact in the world while living a life of simplicity and mindfulness. Whether through financial contributions, volunteering, or raising awareness, minimalist philanthropy allows us to create positive change and make a difference in the lives of others. Embrace minimalist philanthropy as a way to give back with purpose, and discover the joy and fulfilment that comes from making a meaningful impact in the world.

25.EMBRACING MINIMALISM

A Lifetime Journey

I n the journey of minimalist living, the concept of giving back with purpose holds a special place. As we simplify our lives and focus on what truly matters, the act of philanthropy becomes a powerful way to extend our values into the world around us. Minimalist philanthropy is about more than just writing a check or donating goods; it's about cultivating a mindset of generosity and using our resources to make a meaningful impact on the lives of others. In this final chapter, we will explore the principles of minimalist philanthropy, offer practical tips for giving back with purpose, and reflect on the transformative power of generosity in a complex world.

Understanding Minimalist Philanthropy

At its core, minimalist philanthropy is guided by several key principles:

1. **Intentionality**: Minimalist philanthropy involves being intentional about how and where we give. It's about aligning our giving with our values and ensuring that our contributions have a meaningful impact.
2. **Simplicity**: Minimalist philanthropy emphasizes simplicity in our giving practices. It's about focusing on a few key causes or organizations that resonate with us, rather than spreading ourselves too thin.
3. **Mindfulness**: Minimalist philanthropy encourages mindfulness in our giving decisions. It's about taking the time to research and understand the impact of our contributions, ensuring that they are used effectively.
4. **Gratitude**: Minimalist philanthropy cultivates a sense of gratitude for the resources we have and the opportunity to give back. It's about recognizing the privilege we have and using it to make a positive difference in the world.
5. **Leveraging Resources**: Minimalist philanthropy involves leveraging our resources, whether it's time, money, skills, or influence, to create meaningful change. It's about using what we have to contribute to the greater good.

Practical Tips for Minimalist Philanthropy

1. **Define Your Values**: Take the time to reflect on your values and priorities, and identify causes or issues that align with them. This will help you focus your philanthropic efforts and make a greater impact.
2. **Research Charities**: Before making a donation, research charities and organizations to ensure that your contributions will be used effectively. Look for organizations with a proven track record of making a positive impact in their field.
3. **Consider Non-Monetary Contributions**: Don't limit your philanthropy to monetary donations. Consider other ways you can give back, such as volunteering your time, sharing your skills, or advocating for causes you believe in.

4. **Practice Gratitude**: Cultivate a sense of gratitude for the resources you have and the opportunity to give back. This can help you approach philanthropy with a mindset of abundance rather than scarcity.
5. **Share Your Journey**: Consider sharing your philanthropic journey with others. By sharing your experiences and insights, you can inspire others to embrace minimalist philanthropy and make a difference in their own way.

The Transformative Power of Minimalist Philanthropy

Minimalist philanthropy has the power to transform not only the lives of those we help but also our own lives. By giving back with purpose, we can:

- **Deepen Our Connections**: Giving back can strengthen our connections with others, fostering a sense of community and belonging.
- **Find Meaning and Purpose**: Philanthropy can give our lives greater meaning and purpose, as we see the positive impact of our contributions.
- **Inspire Others**: Our acts of generosity can inspire others to give back, creating a ripple effect of kindness and compassion.

In conclusion, minimalist philanthropy is a powerful way to extend the principles of minimalism into our lives and make a meaningful impact on the world around us. By embracing simplicity, intentionality, and mindfulness in our giving practices, we can create positive change and cultivate a more compassionate and generous society. As we continue on our journey of minimalist living, let us remember the transformative power of giving back with purpose and the profound impact it can have on our lives and the world.

Milton Keynes UK
Ingram Content Group UK Ltd.
UKHW051235010424
440421UK00012B/702